EASY GOURMET

Desserts

A STEP·BY·STEP GUIDE

Edited by Charlotte Turgeon

BEEKMAN HOUSE
New York

This 1984 edition is published by Beekman House,
distributed by Crown Publishers, Inc., by arrangement
with Ottenheimer Publishers, Inc.

Library of Congress Catalog Card Number: 82-71717
ISBN: 0-517-381915

h g f e d c b a

Contents

Introduction

A good dessert is the crowning touch to any meal. It leaves a pleasant taste on the palate and a happy feeling about the whole meal, whether it be a family supper or an elegant dinner party. In a sense, carefully prepared desserts are tokens of affection for those we love and compliments to guests that we receive in our homes.

Most desserts are prepared well in advance, leaving the host or hostess free to concentrate on the other courses. Knowing that the sweet finale is ready and waiting is a source of great comfort, especially when you are proud of it. This volume will take you step-by-step through many elegant desserts, but we haven't forgotten good, old fashioned apple pie, home-baked cakes with thick frosting, or the kind of cookies that make a good dessert when served with a glass of cold milk or a cup of cocoa, tea or coffee.

We urge our readers to always remember that a good dessert must be served as attractively as possible. Take time out to garnish and embellish. It is fun to do and always appreciated. An extra flourish with the pastry tube or the addition of fresh flowers or fruit when appropriate will bring rave reviews. Above all, be sure that your pretty dessert bowls and platters are sparkling clean and free from any driblets of frosting or whipped cream. Making a dessert look irresistible is almost as important as making it taste delicious; the combination will be a delight that everyone admires. Bon appétit!

Almond Soufflé (Cold)

People are afraid to make cold soufflés, but this recipe will show how easy it is. This soufflé should be made at least 12 hours in advance.

Yield: 8 Servings

      Shredded almonds
  5 eggs (room temperature)
  ¾ cup sugar
  2 tablespoons rum
  ¾ cup ground almonds
  1 pint heavy cream
  1 tablespoon vanilla extract

3. Separate the eggs into 2 mixing bowls. Add the sugar to the yolks.

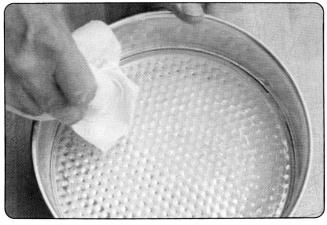

1. Butter a large 9-inch springform mold.

2. Cover the bottom of the mold with shredded almonds.

4. Beat the yolks and sugar with an electric mixer.

CONTINUED

Almond Soufflé *CONTINUED*

5. Beat until the mixture is thick and pale yellow.

8. Pour the cream into a bowl and add the vanilla.

6. Add the rum and stir with a whisk.

9. Beat the cream until stiff.

7. Add the ground almonds and mix well.

10. With a whisk, stir the cream into the egg yolk mixture.

Almond Soufflé

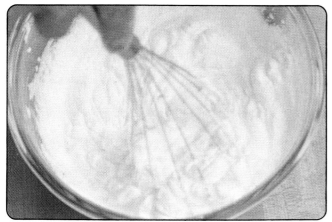

11. Beat the egg whites until stiff but not dry and add a cupful to the egg yolk-cream mixture, stirring gently.

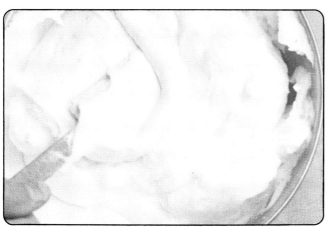

12. Pour the mixture into the remaining egg whites and fold in gently, using a rubber spatula.

13. Pour into the prepared pan.

14. Fold a piece of wax paper into a pointed triangle (like a paper airplane). Place the point in the center and cut at the point the triangle meets the rim of the pan.

15. Unfold the triangle and place the resulting circle over the mold. Place in the freezer for 12 hours.

Banana Rum Soufflé

An orange liqueur or kirsch can substitute for the rum, but only 3 tablespoons are required. You may want to prepare the soufflé dish in advance (see steps 8 and 9). It can be kept in the refrigerator before filling.

Yield: 8 Servings

4 ripe bananas, cut in pieces
2 tablespoons butter
2 tablespoons flour
1 tablespoon sugar
1 cup hot milk
4 tablespoons rum
1 teaspoon vanilla extract
3 egg yolks
5 egg whites (room temperature)

1. Put the bananas in a food processor or food mill.

2. Puree the bananas.

Banana Rum Soufflé

3. Melt the butter in a saucepan and stir in the flour.

6. With a whisk, stir in the hot milk.

4. Add the sugar and mix well.

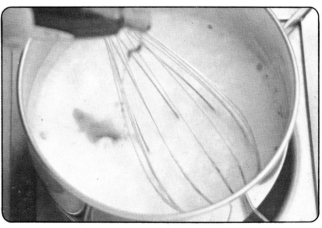

7. Add the rum and vanilla and stir over low heat 2–3 minutes.

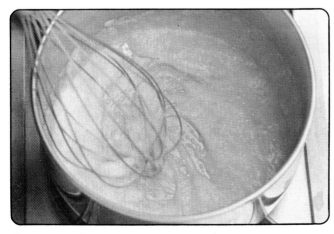

5. Simmer 2–3 minutes, stirring constantly.

8. Butter the bottom and sides of a 2-quart soufflé dish. Sprinkle with sugar.

CONTINUED

Banana Rum Soufflé CONTINUED

9. Turn and tilt the bowl to completely coat the inside of the dish, and shake out any excess sugar.

12. Fold in the bananas thoroughly, using a rubber spatula.

10. Pour the flour mixture into a bowl. Add the egg yolks and stir thoroughly with a whisk.

13. This is the banana soufflé base. Preheat the oven to 375°F.

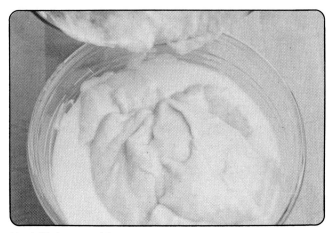

11. Add the pureed bananas.

14. Beat the egg whites until stiff but not dry. Add 2 cups of the beaten egg whites to the soufflé base.

Banana Rum Soufflé

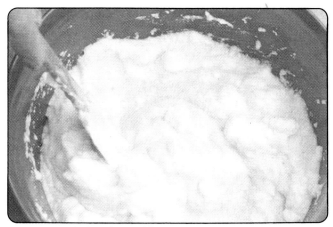

15. Mix gently but thoroughly.

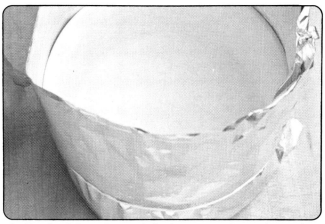

18. Tie the foil in place with kitchen twine. Butter the inside edge of the foil.

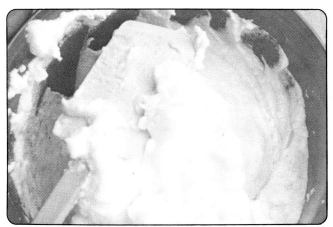

16. Add the remaining egg whites and fold in as described in Step 15 of Chocolate Soufflé (see next recipe).

17. Wrap the mold in a double fold of aluminum foil, so that the top edge is 2–3 inches higher than the mold.

19. Pour the mixture into the soufflé dish and bake 30–40 minutes. Remove the foil and serve immediately, with or without whipped cream.

Chocolate Soufflé

Yield: 8 Servings

1 cup milk
6 tablespoons sugar
2 ounces semi-sweet chocolate
3 tablespoons butter
3 tablespoons flour
4 large egg yolks
6 egg whites

3. Add the chocolate.

1. Pour the milk in a saucepan.

4. Cook over low heat until the chocolate melts, stirring occasionally.

2. Add 2 tablespoons of sugar.

5. Once the chocolate melts, remove the pan from the heat.

Chocolate Soufflé

6. Heat the butter in another saucepan. Add the flour and mix well.

9. Simmer 2–3 minutes, stirring constantly.

7. Stir in the remaining sugar.

10. Pour into a large bowl and add the egg yolks, one by one, beating constantly with a whisk.

8. Add the chocolate mixture.

11. This is the base for the chocolate soufflé. Preheat the oven to 375°F.

CONTINUED

Chocolate Soufflé   CONTINUED

12. Beat the eggs until stiff but not dry. With a whisk, gently stir in 2 cups of the egg whites.

15. Fold the egg whites in gently, cutting down to the bottom of the bowl with a rubber spatula and scooping up the egg whites while turning the bowl. This will keep the egg whites from falling.

13. Mix thoroughly to lighten the soufflé.

16. Pour into a buttered, 2–quart soufflé dish and bake 20–30 minutes, depending on how dry you want the soufflé.

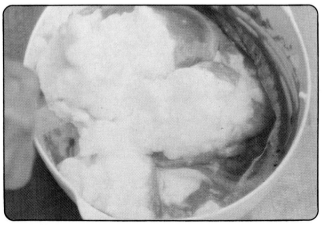

14. Add the rest of the beaten egg whites.

17. Remove from the oven. Sprinkle with confectioners' sugar and serve hot, with or without a bowl of sweetened whipped cream.

Fresh Strawberry Ice

Yield: 8 Servings

1. Put 2 cups of sugar in a saucepan. Add 1 cup of water and the juice of 1 orange. Bring to a boil and cook 3–4 minutes, or until the surface is covered with medium-large bubbles. Remove from the heat.

4. Pour the dissolved gelatin into the pan of syrup.

7. Spin until pureed.

2. In a small bowl, put 2 envelopes of plain gelatin.

5. Put 3 pints of fresh strawberries into a blender or food processor. Add ¼ cup of sugar.

8. Pour the strawberries into a bowl and add the lukewarm syrup gradually, stirring constantly. Pour into a 6–8 cup mold and let stand at least 12 hours in the refrigerator. Unmold and garnish with sweetened whipped cream and fresh strawberries.

3. Stir in ½ cup of cold water to dissolve the gelatin.

6. Add 2 tablespoons of Cointreau or Grand Marnier.

Apple Rum Pudding

Yield: 6 – 8 Servings

6 cooking apples
Juice of ½ lemon
¾ cup brown sugar
1½ tablespoons butter, melted
2 tablespoons cornstarch
¼ cup rum
1 cup water
Cinnamon
1 recipe Brown Sugar Meringue (see next recipe)
2 tablespoons mixed candied fruits

5. Add the melted butter.

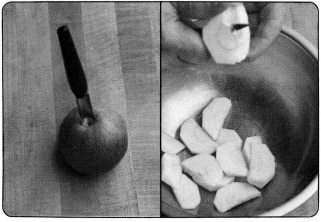

1. Core the apples. 2. Peel the apples and slice them into a bowl.

6. Add the cornstarch.

3. Sprinkle the apples with lemon juice to avoid discoloration. 4. Add the brown sugar.

7. Add the rum and mix well.

Apple Rum Pudding

8. Put the mixture in a saucepan. Cover and cook over moderate heat for 30 minutes. After the first 10 minutes of cooking, add the water.

11. Make the Brown Sugar Meringue and put it in a pastry bag fitted with a medium-large star tip. Decorate the top of the pudding with the meringue.

9. Pour the mixture into a buttered, 9–10 inch oven-proof dish.

12. Sprinkle the top with candied fruit.

10. Sprinkle with cinnamon.

13. Brown 3–4 minutes under the broiler.

Brown Sugar Meringue

1 **lemon**
4 **egg whites**
¼ **cup brown sugar**

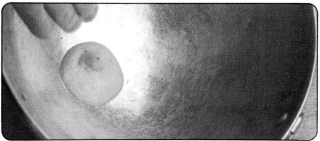

1. Rub a copper or stainless steel bowl with the cut side of a lemon.

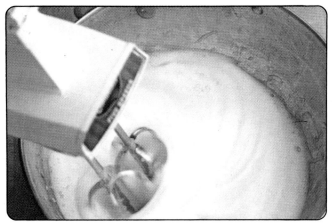

4. Place the bowl upright on the counter and continue beating at top speed until the egg whites are very stiff.

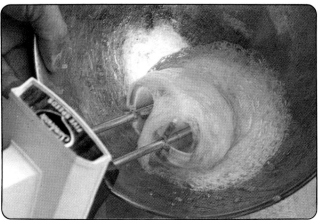

2. Add 4 egg whites (room temperature). Start beating with an electric beater at low speed, tipping the bowl slightly.

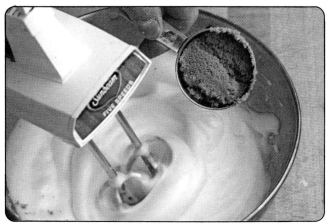

5. Add the brown sugar gradually, beating continuously.

3. Increase the beating speed as the eggs begin to froth.

6. The meringue should be very stiff. Use as a topping in pudding, soufflés, and sweet omelets.

Graham Banana Pudding

The graham crackers can be pulverized in a food processor or crumbled between 2 sheets of wax paper with a rolling pin.

Yield: 6 – 8 Servings

  2 cups milk
  1 tablespoon vanilla extract
  1 cup graham cracker crumbs
  3 eggs (room temperature)
  1 cup brown sugar
  ¼ cup candied fruits
  4 bananas

Preheat the oven to 325°F.

4. Beat the eggs with a hand beater until well blended.

1. Pour the milk into a saucepan and bring to a boil. 2. Stir in the vanilla.

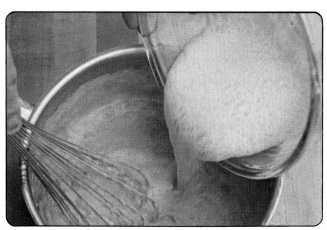

5. Remove the pan from the heat. Add the eggs to the milk-crumb mixture and stir hard.

3. Add the graham cracker crumbs. Stir and simmer 7–8 minutes.

6. Add the brown sugar and mix well.

CONTINUED

Graham Banana Pudding CONTINUED

7. Add the candied fruits.

10. Butter a 9-inch cake pan. Sprinkle with sugar; tilt the pan so that the sugar completely covers the inside. Shake out any excess sugar.

8. Puree the bananas in a food processor or force them through a food mill.

11. Pour the mixture into the pan and bake 1 hour.

9. Combine the bananas with crumb mixture, using a whisk.

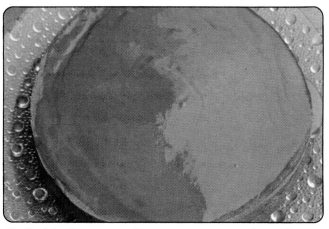

12. Cool for 3 minutes and turn out on a serving platter. Cover with Apricot Sauce (see next recipe).

Apricot Sauce

This sauce is excellent on puddings, unfrosted cakes, and ice cream.

Yield: 2 Cups

1. Put 1 16–ounce can of apricots, with the syrup, into a saucepan.

4. Pour through a strainer.

2. Add ½ cup of sugar.

5. Using a pestle or the back of a spoon, force the apricots through the strainer.

3. Add 1 cup of water and bring to a boil. Cook over moderate heat 8–10 minutes.

6. Stir and serve warm or cold.

Yellow Cake with Chocolate Frosting

This cake is easy to make, yet it can be layered and frosted to look very professional. It can also be left whole and served warm with Citrus Topping.

Yield: 8 – 10 Servings

Cake

   8 eggs (room temperature)
1⅓ cups sugar
   1 tablespoon vanilla extract
   2 cups all-purpose flour

Frosting

 10 ounces semi-sweet chocolate
   1 cup heavy cream
   2 tablespoons hot water
     Confectioners' sugar

Preheat the oven to 300°F.

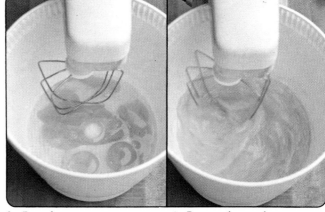

3. Put the eggs in a mixing bowl.

4. Beat with an electric mixer until blended.

1. Butter the bottom and sides of a 10-inch springform pan.

5. Add the sugar gradually, beating at high speed for 3–4 minutes.

2. Sprinkle with flour and tilt the pan to completely cover the inside. Shake out any excess flour.

6. Transfer the batter to a stainless steel bowl and place over a saucepan containing 4 cups of hot (not boiling) water. Beat with a hand electric beater. Make sure that the water is not hot enough to cook the eggs.

Yellow Cake with Chocolate Frosting

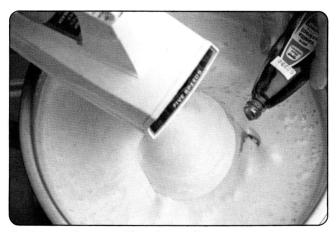

7. Continue beating, adding the vanilla.

10. Gradually sift the flour into the batter, folding it in with a rubber spatula.

8. Here the mixture is not thick enough. Keep beating.

11. Continue to gently fold in the flour, using an upward motion.

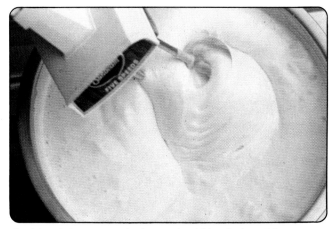

9. After 6–8 minutes, the batter should be thick and 3 times its original volume.

12. Pour the batter into the prepared pan and place on a center rack in the oven. Bake 40–50 minutes or until a cake tester or skewer comes out clean when you penetrate the center.

CONTINUED

Yellow Cake with Chocolate Frosting CONTINUED

13. Unmold on a rack and cool completely. Using a large serrated knife, cut the cake horizontally in half. Set the bottom half to one side.

16. Place the chocolate in a stainless steel bowl. Put it over a saucepan containing 2 cups of boiling water.

14. Slice off the top crust of the cake. This will not be used.

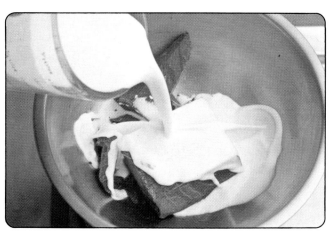

17. Add the cream and heat until the chocolate melts.

15. Cut the remaining cake in 2 layers. You now have 3 layers.

18. Mix with a wooden spoon. If the mixture is too thick, add the hot water.

Yellow Cake
with Chocolate Frosting

19. If the chocolate is not thick enough, continue cooking until it is.

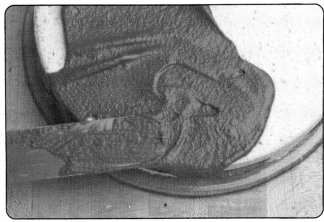

22. Cover with the second layer and spread that with frosting.

20. When the proper consistency is reached, remove from the heat and cool completely, stirring occasionally.

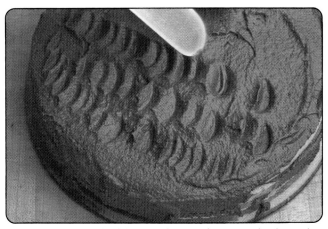

23. Top with the third layer and cover the top and sides with frosting. Make little designs on the top with the spatula.

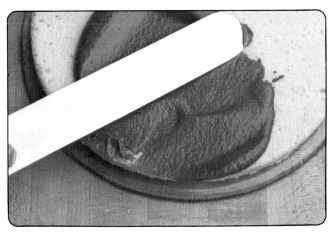

21. Spread the bottom layer with the chocolate frosting.

24. Decorate with the powdered sugar.

Chocolate Cake

Butter a 9-inch springform pan and sprinkle with flour. Tilt the pan to coat the entire interior. Shake out any excess flour.

Yield: 8 Servings

2¼ cups cake flour
1 cup sugar
½ teaspoon salt
½ cup cocoa
2 tablespoons baking powder
½ cup soft, unsalted butter
3 eggs
1½ cups milk

Preheat oven to 325°F.

3. Sift the cocoa and baking powder.

6. Mix the batter at medium speed.

1. Sift the flour and sugar into a mixing bowl.

4. Add the butter and eggs.

7. Beat until the batter is smooth and creamy.

2. Add the salt.

5. Add the milk

8. Pour into the prepared pan and bake 45–60 minutes, or until an inserted cake tester or skewer comes out clean. Turn upside down on a rack and cool completely.

Never Fail Chocolate Frosting

Yield: 1 Cup

3 tablespoons soft butter
3 tablespoons evaporated milk
⅔ cup confectioners' sugar
½ cup cocoa

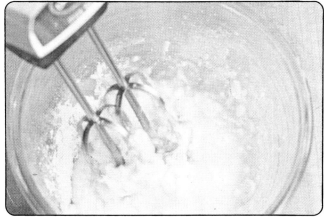

4. Mix with an electric beater until thick and well blended.

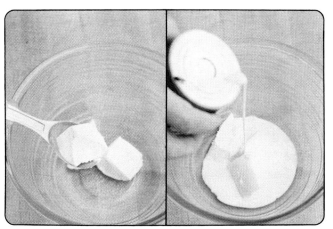

1. Put the softened butter in a mixing bowl. 2. Add the evaporated milk.

5. Add the cocoa and mix well.

3. Add the confectioners' sugar.

6. With a pastry bag fitted with a star tip of whatever size you prefer, you can decorate a cake beautifully.

White Mountain Frosting

2 cups sugar
1 cup water
½ teaspoon cream of tartar
4 egg whites (room temperature)
2 teaspoons vanilla

1. Put the sugar in a heavy saucepan.

4. Bring to a boil without stirring and cook until the syrup measures 240°F on a candy thermometer.

2. Add the water.

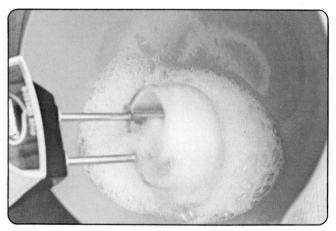

5. Put the egg whites in a stainless steel bowl and beat with an electric mixer.

3. Add the cream of tartar.

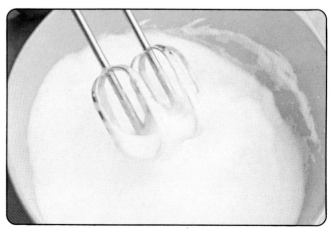

6. Add the vanilla and beat until almost stiff.

White Mountain Frosting

This frosting can be spread on a cake or piped through a pastry bag, and can be tinted a pastel color. It can also be made in advance and stored for several days in the refrigerator.

7. Still beating, start adding the syrup in a fine stream.

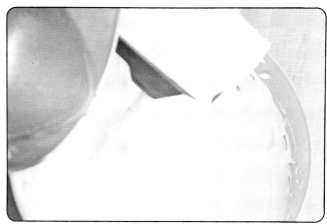

10. Be sure to use all the sugar.

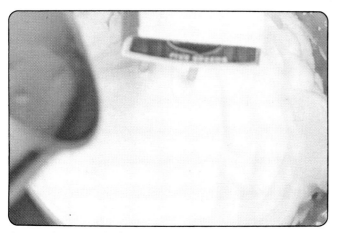

8. Keep beating at high speed.

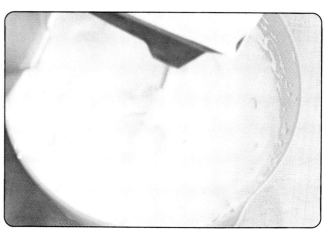

11. It is important to add the syrup very slowly.

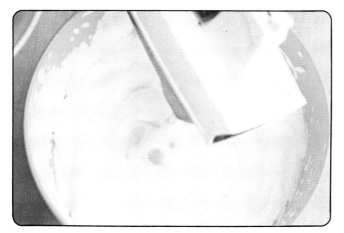

9. The mixture will thicken gradually.

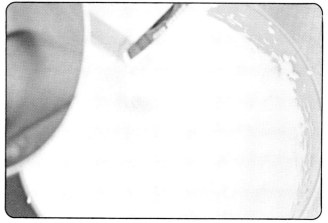

12. When all the syrup is absorbed and the mixture is thick, the frosting is ready. If you want to save the frosting for future use, cover the bowl with a damp towel and store in the refrigerator.

Citrus Topping

This topping is poured lukewarm over Yellow Cake and is decorated with Citrus Garnish (see next recipe).

Yield: 1½ Cups

  1 **cup sugar**
  ¼ **cup cornstarch**
1¼ **cups orange juice**
  3 **tablespoons grated orange and/or lemon rind**
  2 **tablespoons lemon juice**
  2 **tablespoons unsalted butter**
    Citrus garnish

4. Add the orange juice.

1. Put the sugar in a heavy saucepan.   2. Add the cornstarch.

5. Bring to a boil and cook for just 2 minutes, stirring constantly with a whisk.

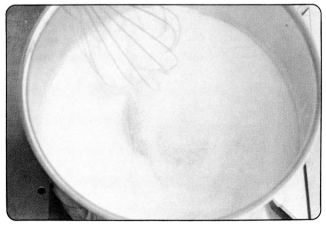

3. Mix well.

6. Add the rind.

Citrus Topping

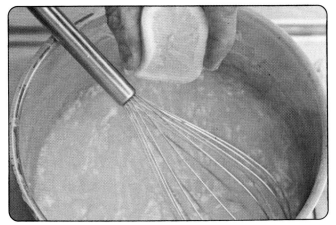

7. Add the lemon juice.

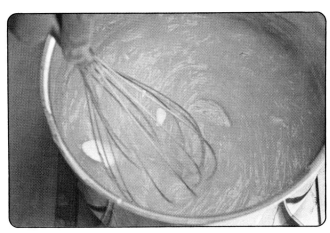

10. Mix with a whisk until the butter melts.

8. If the topping is too thick, add 2 or 3 tablespoons of cold sugar syrup.

11. Pour lukewarm topping over the cake.

9. Add the butter.

12. Sprinkle with Citrus Garnish.

Citrus Garnish

Yield: ¼ Cup

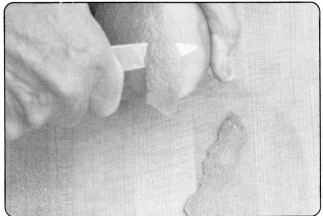

1. Using a very sharp knife, cut off the orange or yellow layer only of an orange or a lemon rind.

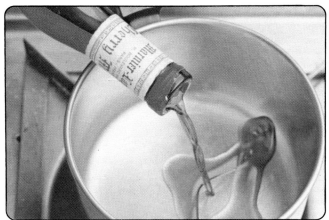

4. Put ¼ cup Grand Marnier or Cointreau and 2 tablespoons of water in a small saucepan.

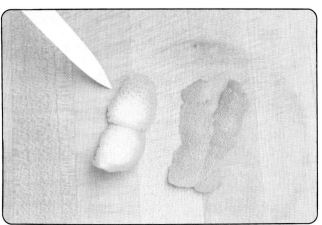

2. Try to avoid the white layer, which is very bitter.

5. Add the rind and bring to a boil.

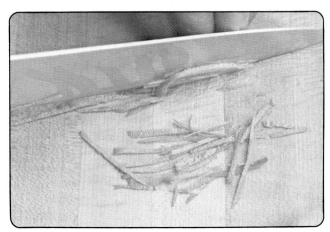

3. Cut the peel into very thin strips.

6. Cook 3 minutes. Spread over the cake just before serving.

Tart and Pie Pastry

One-crust tarts are baked with a pastry ring (which we prefer) or a straight-sided, 8- or 9-inch tin. They are usually filled with fruit and glazed with currant or apricot glaze. The full recipe will make a 9-inch pie. Using wax paper makes rolling out the pastry much easier.

Yield: 2 9-inch crusts

2¾ cups all-purpose flour
1 teaspoon salt
1 tablespoon sugar (optional)
1 cup lard
½ cup (approximately) ice water

3. Measure 1 cup of lard. Some packages come with an indicator on the box.

6. Add the water and mix.

1. Sift the flour and salt into a mixing bowl.

4. Add the lard to the flour and mix.

7. Flours vary: As you can see, this dough is too dry.

2. Using an electric beater, mix the salt and flour with a dough hook. Add sugar if the filling will be sweet.

5. Continue to mix the dough at moderate speed until well blended.

8. Add another tablespoon or two of water if necessary. The moment the mixture starts to form a ball, stop the machine. Form into a ball with your hands. Cover with wax paper and rest for 20 minutes.
CONTINUED

Tart and Pie Pastry CONTINUED

To roll out the pastry

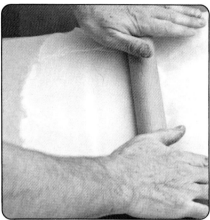

11. When the pastry is 11–12 inches long, turn the paper around so that you can roll in the opposite direction.

14. Roll the pastry up on the pin and unroll it over the pastry ring or pie plate.

9. Place half of the pastry ball between 2 sheets of wax paper.

12. Measure your ring or a pie tin to be sure you have enough pastry, allowing 2–3 inches overhang.

15. Tuck the pastry well into the hollow of the ring or pan and flatten the edges on the rim.

10. Roll out the pastry, leaning lightly but firmly on the rolling pin.

13. Moisten a baking sheet or pie plate with water.

16. For a 1-crust tart, roll the pin over the rim to cut off the excess dough. For pies, follow the directions given in the specific recipe.

Apple Pie

If you've never made a pie, use wax paper when rolling out the pastry. If you are more experienced, you can roll out the pastry on a floured working surface—preferably marble—which can be rubbed with a tray of ice in hot weather. Be sure your rolling pin, as well as your working surface, is as cold as possible.

Yield: 6 – 8 Servings

- 1 recipe Tart and Pie Pastry
- 1 egg beaten with
- 1 teaspoon water
- 6 apples
- 2 teaspoons cinnamon
- ¼ cup brown sugar
- ¼ cup golden raisins (optional)
- 2 tablespoons flour
  Juice of ¼ lemon
- 2 tablespoons confectioners' sugar

3. Roll out the pastry with a lightly floured rolling pin into a large circle about ⅛ inch thick.

6. Tap the bottom and sides with your fingers so that the pastry adheres to the pan well.

1. Put half of the pastry on a lightly floured surface.

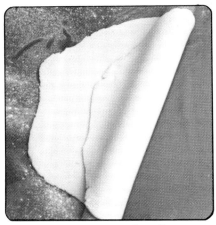

4. Roll the pastry up on the rolling pin.

7. Brush the bottom of the pie with the egg beaten with water.

2. Mold it into a circle with your hands.

5. Unroll it over a 9-inch pie tin.

8. Core and peel the apples.

CONTINUED

Apple Pie CONTINUED

9. Slice the apples and put them in a mixing bowl.

12. Add the raisins, if desired.

15. Fill the pie tin with the apples. Sprinkle with lemon juice and, for a richer pie, dot the surface with 1½ tbsps of butter.

10. Add the cinnamon and brown sugar.

13. Sprinkle with the flour.

16. Brush the pastry rim with cold water.

11. You can substitute white sugar for brown, if desired.

14. Mix everything well. Preheat the oven to 400°F.

17. Cover with the rest of the pastry, rolled out in the same way as the bottom crust.

Apple Pie

18. Pinch the edges together with your fingers.

21. Brush with more of the beaten egg.

22. Sprinkle with confectioners' sugar. Bake 40 minutes.

19. Trim off the edges with a sharp knife.

20. Using the same knife, make little holes all over the surface to allow the steam to escape.

23. Let the pie cool slowly. Serve lukewarm or cool, accompanied with cheese, heavy cream, or vanilla ice cream.

Caramel Custard

Yield: 4 – 6 Servings

Caramel
1½ cups sugar
½ cup water

1. Put the sugar for the caramel in a saucepan. 2. Add the water.

5. Place the pan in a larger pan containing cold water to stop the cooking.

3. Stir with a wooden spoon.

6. Pour the caramel in a 1-quart, straight-sided mold or dessert dish and tilt it in a circular motion so that the bottom and sides are coated.

4. Bring to a boil without stirring. Watch carefully. The moment the syrup turns light brown, remove from the heat.

7. To clean the saucepan, fill it with cold water and cook 7–8 minutes. Pour out and rinse.

Caramel Custard

Preheat the oven to 350°F. Fill a small roasting pan with 1½ cups of hot water and place on the center rack of the oven.

Custard

- 2 cups milk
- ½ cup sugar
- 2 teaspoons vanilla
- 3 whole eggs
- 2 egg yolks

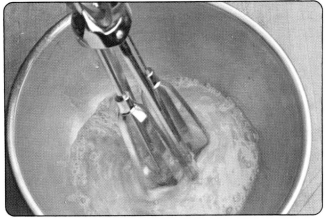

10. Beat the eggs well.

8. Pour the milk into a saucepan. Add the sugar and vanilla. Stir and bring to a boil.

11. Add the hot milk gradually, stirring constantly with a whisk.

9. Put the eggs and egg yolks in a mixing bowl.

12. Pour into the caramel-lined mold and bake 40 minutes. Remove from the oven to cool, then chill in the refrigerator. To serve, the custard dish should be dipped into hot water for a few seconds and turned upside down on a dessert platter. For parties, decorate with candied violets and rosettes of sweetened whipped cream.

Meringue

Meringue is easy to make if you follow directions. It is the basis of many desserts. A meringue cake—which is made with layers of cooked meringue circles—is glued together with uncooked meringue, so always remember to keep some in reserve.

    6 egg whites (room temperature)
      A pinch of salt
      Juice of ½ lemon
 1½ cups sugar
    2 tablespoons cornstarch (optional)

Preheat the oven to 170°F.

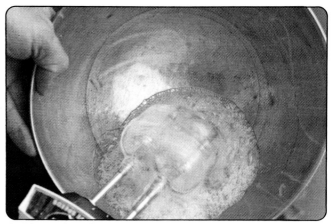

2. Using a hand beater and tilting the bowl slightly, start beating slowly. Avoid letting the beater touch the bottom of the bowl.

3. Once the eggs begin to froth, increase the speed of the beater.

1. Put the egg whites in a bowl. Add the salt and lemon juice.

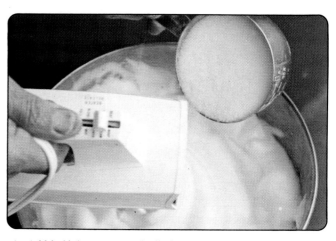

4. Add half the sugar, gradually beating at top speed.

Meringue

5. When the meringue is really stiff, add the remaining sugar and the cornstarch if a more cake-like texture is preferred.

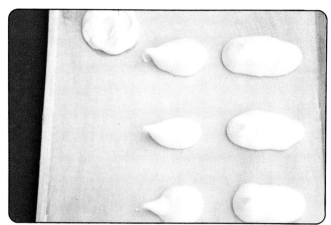

9. Or, make small circular bases.

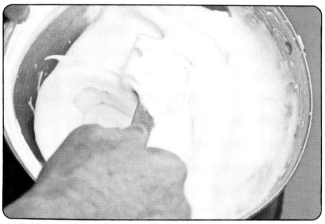

6. Fold in with a rubber spatula, using an upward motion and turning the bowl at the same time. This keeps the egg whites from falling.

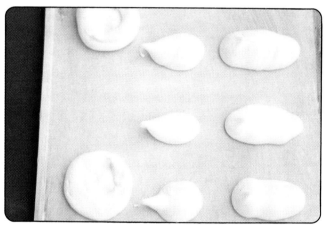

10. Put a rim around the bases to make small baskets.

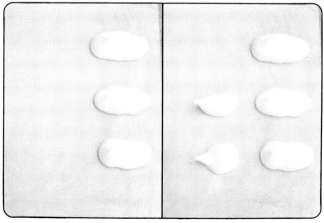

7. Put the meringue in a pastry bag, fitted with a plain tip. Butter an aluminum baking dish and dust it with flour. Pipe small eclairs onto the sheet.

8. Or, make small cream puffs.

11. If you prefer, use a star tip and make the shapes more decorative. Cook for 2 hours in a 170°F oven.

Pear Meringue Cake

This is a great party dessert. Make the meringue basket in advance and assemble shortly before serving.

Preheat oven to 170°F.

Yield: 6 – 8 Servings

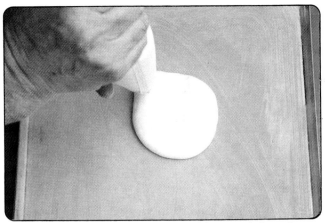

1. Butter an aluminum baking sheet and dust it with flour. Starting at the center, pipe a spiral, using a pastry bag fitted with a plain tip.

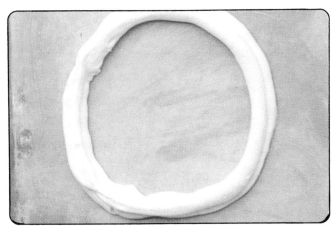

4. Follow the line of the circles with the pastry bag, forcing enough meringue out to make the meringue rounds thick.

2. Continue the spiral until it measures 8 or 9 inches. Bake 2 hours.

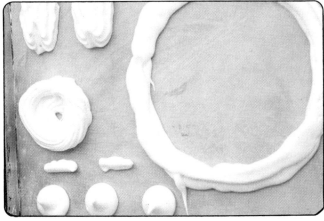

5. Make 3 little mushroom caps and 3 little stems to use as decoration. Remember to save some uncooked meringue for "glue" and for frosting the basket. Bake 2 hours. Cool completely.

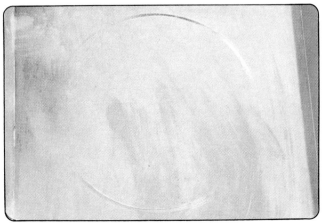

3. Next, you will be making the walls of the basket. Butter and flour another large baking sheet. Place an 8- or 9-inch layer-cake tier upside down on the sheet to trace 2 perfect circles.

6. To make the basket, place the cooked base on a platter. Pipe little mounds of uncooked meringue around the rim of the base.

Pear Meringue Cake

7. Place a ring on the base, pressing it down gently but firmly.

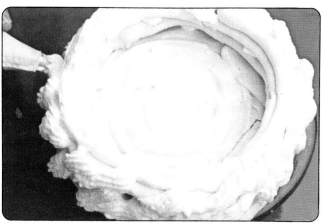

10. "Frost" the outside, using a decorative tip and making whatever designs you fancy.

8. Dot the ring with more uncooked meringue and top with the second ring.

11. Sprinkle with praline.

9. The rings are now in place.

12. Put 6 or 7 well-drained canned pear halves in the basket.

CONTINUED

Pear Meringue Cake CONTINUED

13. Sprinkle with candied fruit.

16. Put in the stems, gluing them with meringue or whipped cream.

14. Decorate with sweetened whipped cream.

17. Place the little mushrooms on the whipped cream.

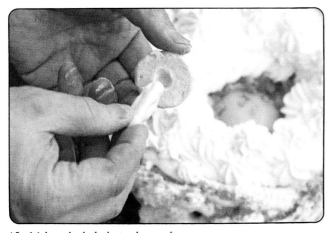

15. Make a little hole in the mushroom caps.

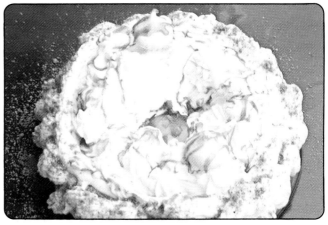

18. Sprinkle with more praline or burnt sugar.

Peach Meringue Baskets with Caramel

Have all the elements of this recipe ready for last-minute assembly.

Yield: 8 Servings

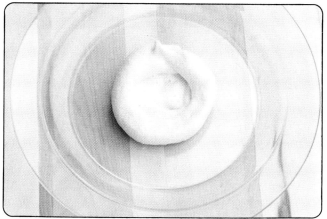

1. Make 8 individual meringue baskets as described in the preceding recipe. Put them on individual dessert plates.

2. Place half a peach (cooked or canned) in each basket.

3. Top with cold, sweetened whipped cream.

4. Pour a thin stream of caramel on top.

5. To make the caramel, put 1 cup of sugar in a small metal saucepan.

6. Add ¼ cup of water. Swirl the sugar and water, but do not stir. Cook over medium heat, watching carefully until it turns light brown. Place the pan in a large pan of cold water to stop the cooking. Keep lukewarm over hot (not boiling) water. To serve, pour the caramel in a very fine stream over the dessert.

42

Lady Fingers

You'll need 3 bowls for this recipe. Have the eggs at room temperature.

Yield: About 5 dozen

6 eggs (separated)
½ cup sugar
1 teaspoon vanilla extract
⅔ cup cake flour
Pinch of salt
1 cup sifted confectioners' sugar

Preheat the oven to 300°F.

4. Sift the cake flour twice and put it in a mixing bowl.

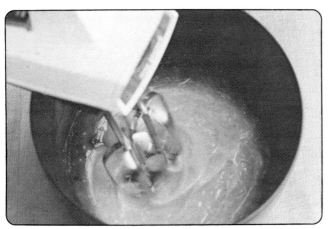
1. Separate the egg whites from the yolks. Beat the egg yolks with an electric mixer for 30 seconds.

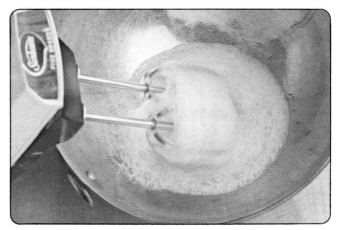
5. Put the egg whites in a stainless steel bowl and beat to a froth. Add the salt.

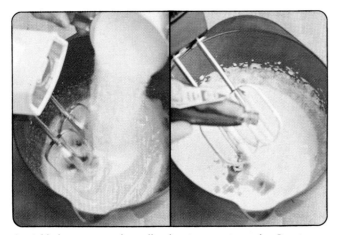
2. Add the sugar to the yolks, beating continuously. Continue beating 4 minutes more at top speed.
3. Add the vanilla and beat.

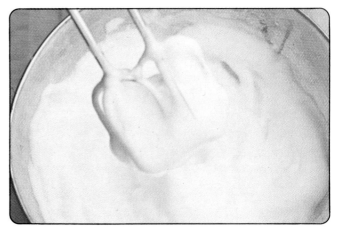
6. Beat the egg whites until stiff.

Lady Fingers

7. Add ¼ of the beaten egg whites to the yolks. Fold in gently.

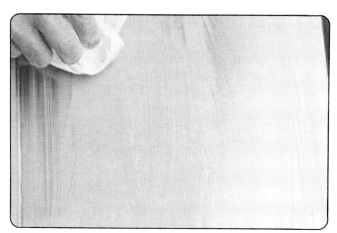

10. Butter an aluminum baking sheet.

8. Add ¼ of the flour and fold in.

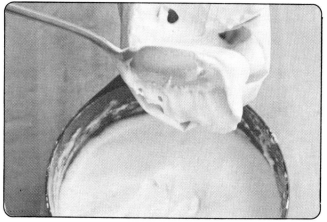

11. Fill a large pastry bag—fitted with a plain medium-size tip—with the batter.

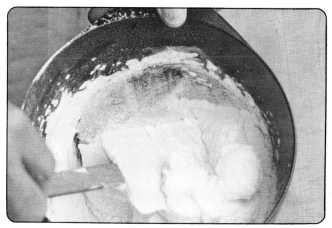

9. Continue adding first the egg whites, then the flour, until all are incorporated.

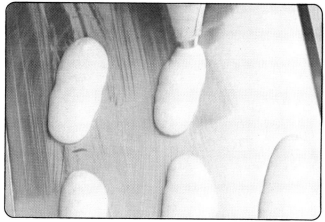

12. Pipe 3-inch-long lady fingers on the baking sheet, 2 inches apart. Sprinkle with the confectioners' sugar. Turn the sheet over and tap to remove excess sugar (the lady fingers will not fall off). Bake 30 minutes on a center rack.

Coconut Macaroons

When you are baking cookies, you will get the best results if you use a permanently shiny aluminum pan. Always preheat the oven.

Yield: About 5 dozen

½ cup sweetened condensed milk
2 cups coconut, shredded
1 teaspoon vanilla extract
1 tablespoon lemon rind, grated
2 egg whites
   Pinch of salt

Preheat oven to 350°F.

4. Add the vanilla and continue beating.

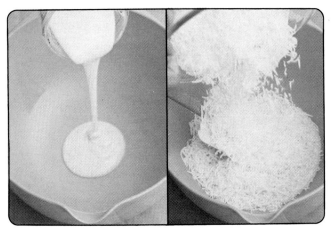

1. Pour the milk into a mixing bowl.   2. Add the shredded coconut.

5. It is important to mix with a spatula and not with an electric beater.

3. Mix with a spatula.

6. Add the lemon rind.

Coconut Macaroons

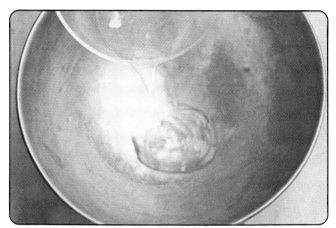

7. Put the egg whites in a copper or stainless steel bowl. If you are using stainless steel, rub the bowl with the cut side of a lemon.

10. When the egg whites are stiff enough to form peaks, they are ready.

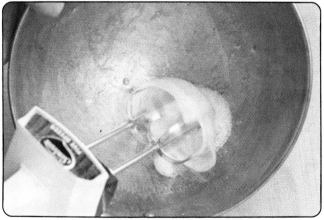

8. Tip the bowl and beat the eggs with an electric hand beater at slow speed until they froth.

11. Fold the egg whites into the coconut mixture.

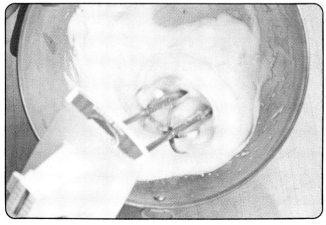

9. Once they begin to thicken, add a pinch of salt and set the bowl upright on the counter. Continue beating at top speed.

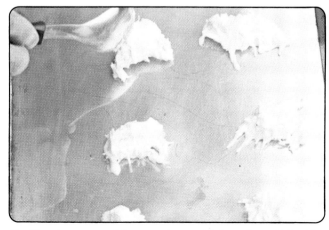

12. Drop by teaspoonfuls onto a buttered baking sheet. Bake 15 minutes.

Nut Kisses

Yield: About 40 kisses

  3 egg whites
    Pinch of salt
  1 cup sugar
 ½ **teaspoon cream of tartar**
  1 teaspoon vanilla extract
1½ **cups walnuts, chopped**

Preheat the oven to 300°F.

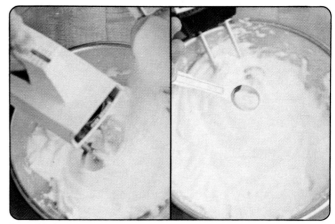

3. Add the sugar gradually, still beating.

4. Add the cream of tartar and continue to beat.

1. Put the egg whites in a stainless steel bowl. Start beating slowly until the eggs froth.

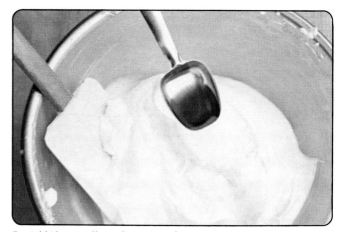

5. Add the vanilla and continue beating.

2. Add a pinch of salt and continue beating until the eggs are very stiff.

6. Fold in the nuts with a rubber spatula. Drop tablespoonfuls of the mixture onto a buttered and floured aluminum baking sheet, leaving an inch between each cookie. Bake 20 minutes.

Oatmeal Cookies

Yield: About 50, 2-inch cookies

1 cup all-purpose flour
1 teaspoon baking powder
  Pinch of salt
½ teaspoon baking soda
⅔ cup vegetable oil
1 cup brown sugar (firmly packed)
2 eggs
1 teaspoon vanilla extract
½ cup coconut, shredded
1¼ cups quick-rolled oats

Preheat the oven to 350°F.

4. Pour the oil into a mixing bowl.

1. Sift the flour onto wax paper.   2. Sift the baking powder onto the flour.

5. Add the brown sugar.

3. Sift the salt and baking soda onto the flour mixture.

6. Mix 2–3 minutes with an electric beater on medium speed.

CONTINUED

Oatmeal Cookies CONTINUED

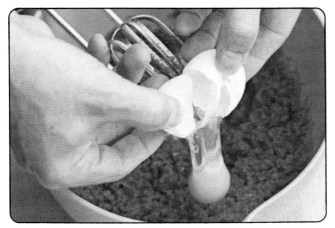

7. Add 1 whole egg.

10. Fold the dry ingredients into the egg mixture with a rubber spatula.

8. Continue mixing 2–3 minutes.

11. Add the vanilla and stir well.

9. Resift the dry ingredients.

12. Add the coconut and continue mixing with a spatula.

Oatmeal Cookies

13. Here the mixture is too thick.

16. Finally, add the oatmeal flakes.

14. Add another egg.

17. Fold in completely with a spatula.

15. Beat well with an electric beater for 2 minutes.

18. Drop the batter through a pastry bag fitted with a large tip or from a teaspoon onto a well-buttered, aluminum baking sheet. Bake 10–12 minutes.

Candied Fruit Cookies

Yield: 30 – 40, 3-inch cookies

  1 cup unsalted butter, softened
1½ cups sugar
  4 whole eggs
  1 teaspoon vanilla
  3 cups cake flour, sifted
  1 teaspoon baking soda
  1 cup mixed candied fruits, diced
  1 cup golden raisins
  2 teaspoons cinnamon
 ½ teaspoon nutmeg

Preheat oven to 350°F.

4. Add the eggs, one by one, beating hard with an electric beater after each addition.

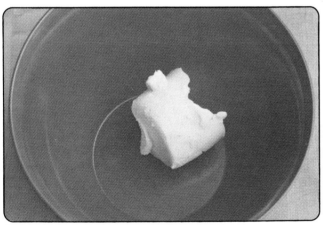

1. Put the butter in a mixing bowl.

5. Continue beating for 2 minutes.

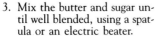

2. Add the sugar.

3. Mix the butter and sugar until well blended, using a spatula or an electric beater.

6. Beat in the vanilla.

Candied Fruit Cookies

7. Sift the flour into the bowl.

10. Add the candied fruit and stir.

8. Stir well.

11. Add the raisins, cinnamon, and nutmeg. Stir well.

9. Add the baking soda and fold in with a rubber spatula.

12. Butter an aluminum baking sheet. Drop the batter by tablespoons onto the sheet, allowing 2 inches between each cookie. Bake 12–15 minutes.

Chocolate Chip Cookies

1 cup all-purpose flour
1 teaspoon baking powder
¼ teaspoon baking soda
Pinch of salt
½ cup walnuts, chopped
⅓ cup unsalted butter
1 cup brown sugar, firmly packed
1 teaspoon vanilla extract
1 egg, well beaten
½ cup chocolate chips

Preheat oven to 350°F.

4. It is important to sift the flour to eliminate any hard lumps.

1. Sift the flour into a mixing bowl.

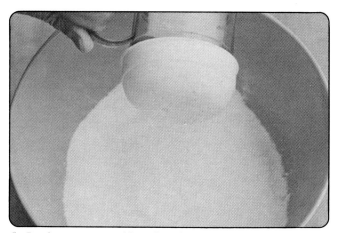

5. Resift once more, adding the salt.

2. Add the baking powder. 3. Add the baking soda.

6. Add the chopped nuts.

Chocolate Chip Cookies

7. Mix everything well.

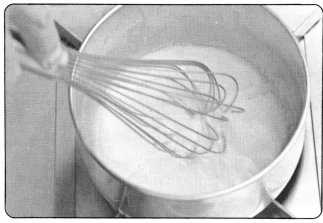

10. Once the butter is melted, remove from heat.

8. Melt the butter over low heat.

11. With a spoon, remove the whey that floats to the surface. You now have clarified butter.

9. Stir with a whisk while the butter is melting.

12. Add the brown sugar.

CONTINUED

Chocolate Chip Cookies

13. Stir with a whisk until blended.

14. Stir in the vanilla.

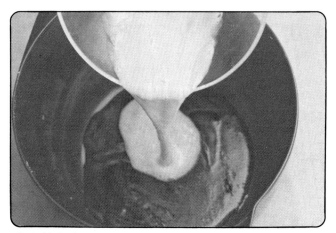

15. Add the beaten egg.

16. Mix with an electric beater, using medium speed.

17. Add the flour mixture and blend well with a rubber spatula.

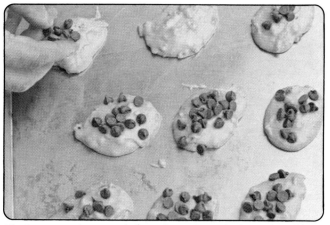

18. Butter an aluminum baking sheet. Drop the batter by tablespoons, 2 inches apart, onto the sheet. Sprinkle with chocolate chips and bake 20–25 minutes.

Jam Cookies

Use your favorite marmalade or jam for these cookies or use a variety of jams. The different colors are very pretty on a cookie platter.

Yield: About 30, 2-inch cookies

- ½ cup vegetable oil
- ¾ cup brown sugar
- 1 whole egg
- 1 teaspoon vanilla
- 1½ cups cake flour
- 1 tablespoon baking powder
   Pinch of salt
- 1 cup walnuts, chopped
   Marmalade or jam

Preheat the oven to 350°F.

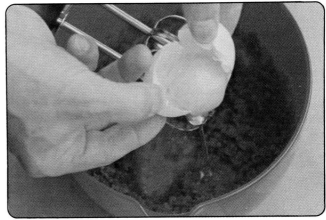
4. Add the egg.

1. Put the oil in a mixing bowl. 2. Add the brown sugar.

5. Beat until thick and creamy.

3. Mix with an electric beater.

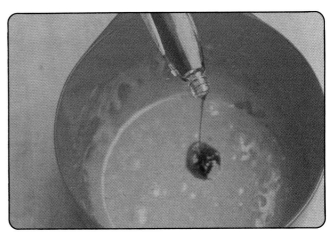
6. Add the vanilla and mix well.

CONTINUED

Jam Cookies CONTINUED

7. Sift the flour into a bowl.

10. Mix well with a rubber spatula.

8. Sift in the baking powder and salt.

11. The mixture is now thick enough to form cookies.

9. Add the chopped nuts.

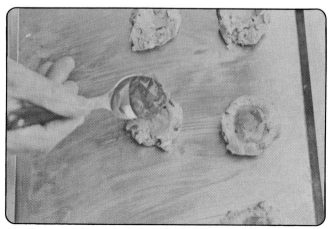

12. Butter an aluminum baking sheet and dust with flour. Place little balls of dough 2 inches apart on the sheet. Press in the centers with your finger to make little wells. Put marmalade or jam in the wells and bake 12–15 minutes.

Tart Pastry

Fruit tarts make a delicious dessert. The pastry shell can be filled with all kinds of fresh fruit in season—pears, peaches, strawberries, grapes, etc. Red fruits are usually glazed with lukewarm currant jelly. The paler fruits are glazed with their own cooking syrup or apricot jam that has been strained and heated to lukewarm. This recipe will make 2 tart shells—if only 1 is desired, halve the pastry and wrap the unused dough in plastic wrap. It will keep for days in the refrigerator.

Yield: 2 Tart Shells

2⅔ cups all-purpose flour
1 cup confectioners' sugar
1½ teaspoons salt
½ cup vegetable shortening
½ cup unsalted butter
2 whole eggs
1 teaspoon vanilla extract
⅓ cup milk or cream

Glaze

1 egg beaten with 1 teaspoon water

Preheat the oven to 375°F.

4. Add the vegetable shortening.

1. Sift the flour into a mixing bowl.

5. Add the butter.

2. Add the confectioners' sugar. 3. Add the salt.

6. Mix well with the dough hook of an electric beater for just 2 minutes.

CONTINUED

Tart
Pastry CONTINUED

7. Add the eggs.

10. Add the milk or cream to soften the dough.

8. Add the vanilla.

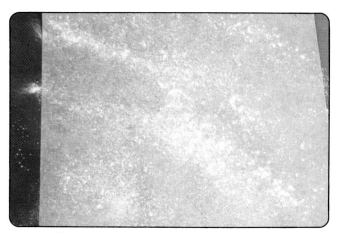

11. Sprinkle a piece of wax paper with flour.

9. Mix with the dough hook just until the dough forms a ball.

12. Place half the pastry on the paper.

Tart
Pastry

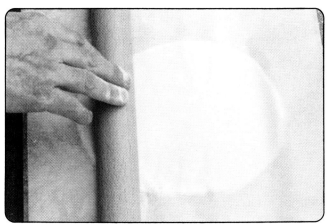

13. Cover the dough with another piece of wax paper.

16. Using a dry paint brush, remove any excess flour.

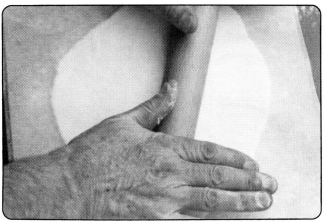

14. Leaning lightly on the roller, roll out the dough into a circle, approximately 12 inches in diameter and ⅛ inch thick.

17. Roll the pastry up on the rolling pin and unroll onto a lightly buttered, 8-9 inch tart ring or straight-sided tart tin.

15. When the pastry is the desired size, remove the top piece of wax paper.

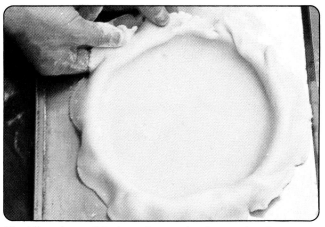

18. Allow about a 2-inch overhang and make sure that the pastry fits well into the bottom of the tart. Do not stretch the pastry.

CONTINUED

Tart Pastry *CONTINUED*

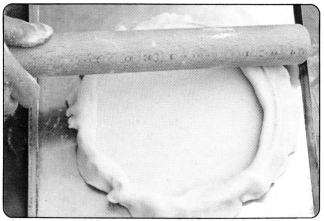

19. Fold 1½ inches of the pastry toward the inside of the rim before running the roller over the rim to cut off excess pastry.

22. Brush the bottom of the pastry with the egg mixture.

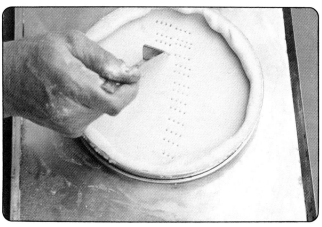

20. Turn up the edge of the pastry and prick the bottom repeatedly with a fork.

23. Brush the inside sides of the tart shell and the outside of the exposed rim.

21. Beat the egg with the water.

24. Fill the tart shell with tiny lead weights or with dried beans to prevent the crust from rising while it cooks. Cook at 375°F for 30 minutes.

Fresh Pear Tart

Prepare the Tart Pastry, Pastry Cream, and Sweetened Whipped Cream before assembling this dessert.

Yield: 6 – 8 Servings

4-6 pears (ripe but very firm)
  3 cups cold water
  1 cup sugar
  2 teaspoons vanilla extract
  1 Tart Pastry
1½ cups Pastry Cream
    Sweetened Whipped Cream

4. Pour the water into a large, flat-bottomed saucepan.

1. Cut the top and bottom of the pears.   2. Remove the cores with a coring knife.

5. Add the sugar.

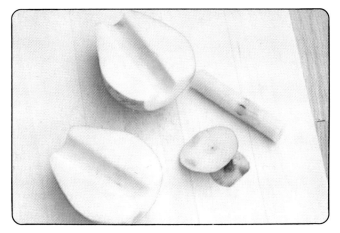

3. Peel the pears and cut in half.

6. Add the vanilla and bring to a boil. Cook uncovered 4–5 minutes.

CONTINUED

Fresh Pear Tart CONTINUED

7. When the bubbles are quite large, the syrup has reached the proper stage.

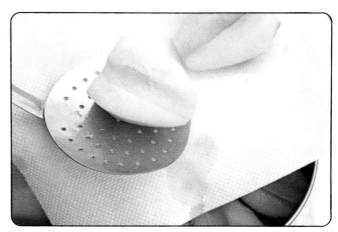

10. Drain the pears on a paper towel.

8. Add the pear halves and cook over medium heat for 5–6 minutes.

11. Cut the pears into 5 or 6 slices, according to their size.

9. When an inserted knife comes out easily, the pears are cooked. Remove them from the heat and let them cool in the syrup.

12. The pears are now ready to go into the tart.

Fresh Pear Tart

13. Cover the bottom of the pastry with Pastry Cream.

16. Fill in the corners with a slice of pear.

14. Cover the pastry cream with uniform lines of pear slices.

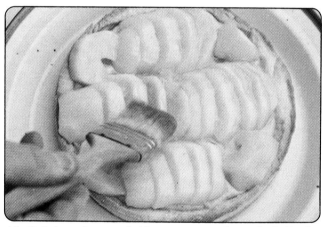

17. Boil down the syrup 8–10 minutes or until very thick. Brush the pears with the syrup or substitute lukewarm, sieved apricot jam.

15. Here are the pears in position.

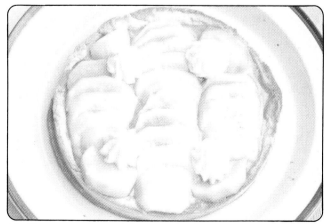

18. Decorate with piped Sweetened Whipped Cream.

Cream Puff Pastry

Yield: 16 large puffs or 24 eclairs

1. Pour 1 cup of water into a saucepan and add 7 tablespoons of unsalted butter.

4. Put 1 cup of all-purpose flour all at once into the saucepan and add ⅛ teaspoon of salt.

7. When the dough no longer sticks to the saucepan or to the spoon, it is cooked.

2. Bring to a boil and simmer 2 minutes.

5. Stir vigorously with a wooden spoon.

8. Transfer the dough to a bowl.

3. The butter will melt completely.

6. Cook 2 minutes, stirring hard.

9. Add a large, unbeaten egg.

Cream Puff Pastry

10. Beat with a wooden spoon or an electric beater using a dough hook until well mixed.

13. After the addition of the fourth egg, the dough should be neither too thick nor too runny.

16. Dip a fork in 1 whole egg beaten with 1 teaspoon of water and lightly flatten each cream puff. Preheat the oven to 375°F.

11. Repeat the process with 3 more large eggs.

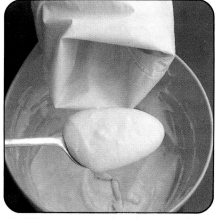

14. Fill a large pastry bag that is fitted with a medium-size plain tip.

17. Let the cream puff or eclairs stand 20 minutes before putting them into the oven. Bake 25–30 minutes according to the size of the puffs. They should be light golden brown and sound hollow if you tap them.

12. After the addition of the third egg, the dough should be very thick.

15. To make cream puffs or eclairs, pipe them out on a buttered and floured, aluminum baking sheet in the desired shape or size.

18. Turn off the heat and keep the oven door ajar. Let the puffs dry for 1 hour to keep them from falling.

Pastry Cream

5 egg yolks
½ cup sugar
½ cup (scant) all-purpose flour
1¾ cups milk
1 teaspoon vanilla extract
2 tablespoons liqueur (orange, kirsch, raspberry, or rum), optional
1 tablespoon unsalted butter

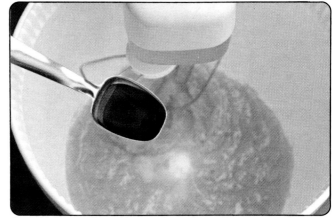

3. Add the vanilla and beat with an electric beater at medium speed for 2–3 minutes.

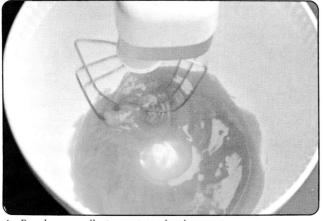

1. Put the egg yolks in a mixing bowl.

4. Meanwhile, heat the milk over medium heat.

2. Add the sugar.

5. Add the flour to the egg-sugar mixture and mix thoroughly.

Pastry Cream

6. Add the liqueur, if desired. Mix well.

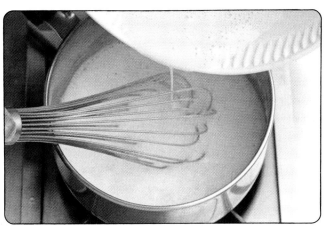

9. Pour the egg mixture into the saucepan, stirring constantly with a whisk.

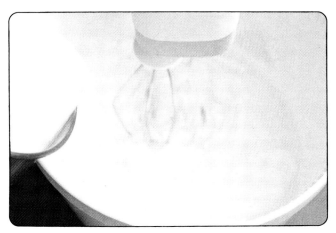

7. Add half the milk to the mixture.

10. Cook over low heat, stirring constantly.

8. Put the rest of the milk back over the heat.

11. The mixture will begin to thicken.

CONTINUED

Pastry Cream CONTINUED

12. The pastry cream will turn pale gold.

13. When the pastry cream forms a ribbon when dripped from a spoon, remove from the heat.

14. Stir in the butter.

15. Pour the mixture into a bowl.

16. Brush a film of butter on the top to prevent a crust from forming.

17. Place wax paper directly over the cream.

Sweetened Whipped Cream

Yield: 4 Cups

1 pint heavy cream
2 teaspoons vanilla extract
¼ cup confectioners' sugar
   Extra confectioners' sugar for decoration

3. Beat at medium speed with an electric beater until stiff.

1. Pour the cream into a stainless steel bowl.

4. Sift in the confectioners' sugar.

2. Add the vanilla.

5. Beat 30 seconds. Sprinkle with confectioners' sugar.

French Cream Puff Cake

You can make the Pastry Cream and the Cream Puff Pastry 2 or 3 days in advance. The cream puff cake can be kept wrapped for 3 days at room temperature. The whole dessert can be assembled 4 hours before serving. See the preceding recipes for making Cream Puff Pastry, Pastry Cream, and Sweetened Whipped Cream.

Preheat oven to 375°F.

1. Butter an aluminum baking sheet.

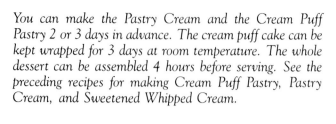

4. Using a 10-inch pastry ring or tart pan, trace a circle on the flour.

2. Dust the sheet with flour.

5. Follow the Cream Puff Pastry recipe through step 14. Preheat the oven to 375°F.

3. Remove the excess flour from the sheet by hitting it against the counter.

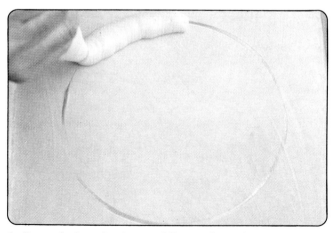

6. Pipe a thick circle of pastry following the outline.

French Cream
Puff Cake

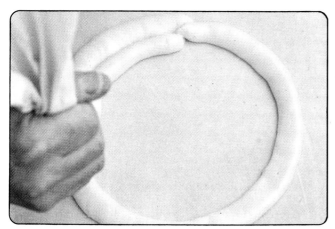

7. Make a second circle inside the first.

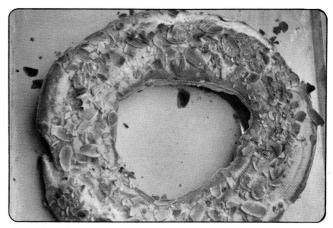

10. Bake 1 hour. Turn off the heat and keep the door slightly ajar. Let the cake dry for 1 hour. This is very important.

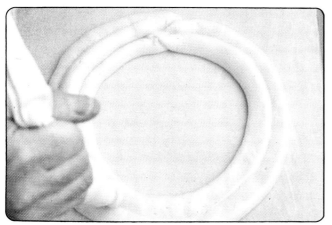

8. Make a third circle on top of the other two.

11. Slide the sharp blade of a knife through the ring, cutting it in half horizontally.

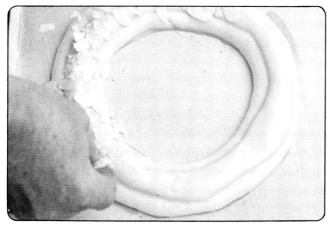

9. Paint twice with a whole egg beaten with 1 teaspoon of water, flattening the circles very slightly. Sprinkle well with sliced almonds.

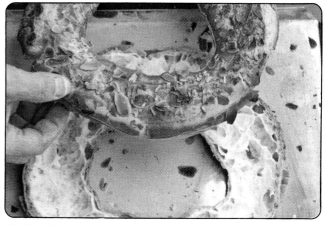

12. Set the top ring aside.

CONTINUED

French Cream
Puff Cake CONTINUED

13. Fill the bottom half with the Pastry Cream, flavored as desired.

16. Cover with the top half and dust with confectioners' sugar.

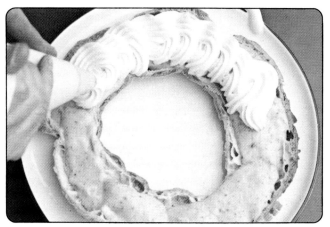

14. Pipe the Sweetened Whipped Cream in thick swirls over the Pastry Cream.

17. Garnish with fresh-picked daisies.

15. The cream should look like this.

Dessert Crêpes

These can be made in advance and stored in packages of 6–8 in the freezer. Allow 15 minutes for thawing.

Yield: 28 – 30 Crêpes

1. Sift 1½ cups of all-purpose flour and ¼ teaspoon of salt into a mixing bowl.

3. Add 6 whole eggs.

2. Add 4 tablespoons of sugar.

4. Add 1½ cups of milk.

CONTINUED

Dessert Crêpes CONTINUED

5. Mix with a whisk or an electric beater until smooth.

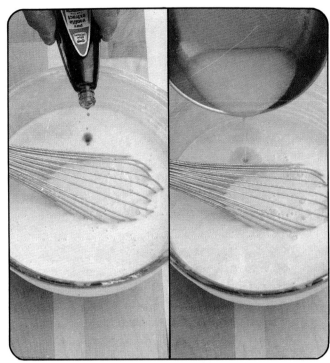

7. Add 1 teaspoon of vanilla extract.

8. Add 3 tablespoons of cooled melted butter.

6. Add ¼ cup of rum.

9. Strain into another bowl. Cover with plastic wrap and refrigerate for at least 1 hour before cooking. Butter or oil a crêpe pan and heat the pan over moderate heat. Pour a little batter in the corner of the pan. Shake the pan gently until the batter completely covers the bottom. Cook for 1 minute. Turn the crêpe over with a spatula and cook briefly. Pile the crêpes on a plate, with a little sugar sprinkled between each crêpe.

Apple Crêpes with Maple Syrup

Prepare the Dessert Crêpes in advance.

Yield: 4 Servings

1. Peel and core 2 large Golden Delicious apples. Heat 2 tablespoons of butter in a skillet and slice the apples into the hot butter.

4. Add 1 tablespoon of maple syrup and continue cooking 3–4 minutes.

2. Add ¼ cup of brown sugar and mix well. Cook over medium heat for 2–3 minutes, tossing the apples frequently.

5. Place some of the filling in each crêpe and roll them up. Place on a buttered oven-proof serving dish.

3. Add the juice of ½ lemon.

6. Garnish with the rest of the apples. Sprinkle with a little brown sugar and maple syrup. Bake in a 350°F oven for 4–5 minutes, or longer if the stuffed crêpes have been prepared in advance. If desired, pour ¼ cup of hot rum over the surface and ignite just before serving.

Sweet Banana Crêpes

Prepare and cook the crêpes in advance.

1. Place 1 tablespoon of unsalted butter and 1 tablespoon of sugar in a small skillet and cook over medium heat for 1 minute.

4. Mix 1 teaspoon of cornstarch and 1 tablespoon of cold water. Add ½ cup of rum, if desired. Stir gently until the sauce thickens.

2. Add 2 thickly sliced bananas and cook 1 minute, turning the bananas once.

5. Put 3–4 slices of banana and a little sauce in each crêpe. Fold in half and then in quarters.

3. Add the juice of 2 oranges and ½ lemon and cook 1 more minute.

6. Put 2 crêpes on each individual, lightly buttered, oven-proof serving dish. Put a tablespoon of orange marmalade or strawberry jam on each crêpe. Sprinkle with powdered sugar and bake 3 minutes at 400°F. Allow extra time if the crêpes have been prepared in advance.